POINT OF IMPACT

# The Emancipation Proclamation

## The Abolition of Slavery

JANET RIEHECKY

Heinemann Library
Chicago, Illinois

© 2002 Reed Educational & Professional Publishing
Published by Heinemann Library,
an imprint of Reed Educational & Professional Publishing,
Chicago, Illinois

Customer Service  888-454-2279

Visit our website at www.heinemannlibrary.com

Produced for Heinemann Library by Discovery Books Limited
Designed by Sabine Beaupré
Illustrations by Stefan Chabluk
Originated by Ambassador Litho Limited
Printed in Hong Kong

06 05 04 03 02
10 9 8 7 6 5 4 3 2 1

**Library of Congress Cataloging-in-Publication Data**
Riehecky, Janet, 1953-
    The Emancipation Proclamation : The abolition of slavery / Janet
Riehecky.
        p. cm. -- (Point of impact)
Includes bibliographical references and index.
Summary: Examines the issue of slavery in the United States and the rift
it created between states and explores the circumstances leading up to
the Emancipation Proclamation, and the impact of the abolition of
slavery.
    ISBN 1-58810-556-3 (lib. bdg.)          ISBN 1-4034-0071-7 (pbk. bdg.)
    1.  United States. President (1861-1865 : Lincoln). Emancipation
Proclamation--Juvenile literature. 2.  Lincoln, Abraham,
1809-1865--Juvenile literature. 3.  Slaves--Emancipation--United
States--Juvenile literature. 4.  Slavery--United States--History--19th
century--Juvenile literature. 5.  United States--Politics and
government--1861-1865--Juvenile literature. 6.  United States--Politics
and government--19th century--Juvenile literature. [1. Emancipation
Proclamation. 2. Slavery--History. 3. United States--History--Civil War,
1861-1865.] I. Title. II. Series.
    E453 .R54 2002
    973.7'14--dc21
                                        2001003480

**Acknowledgments**
The author and publishers are grateful to the following for permission to reproduce copyright material:
Corbis, pp. 5, 6, 7, 8, 9, 10, 11, 12, 13, 14, 15, 16, 17, 18, 20, 21, 22, 23, 24, 25, 26, 27, 28, 29;
The Granger Collection, p. 4.

Cover photographs reproduced with permission of Corbis.

Some words are shown in bold, **like this.** You can find out what they mean by looking in the glossary.

# Contents

# January 1, 1863

## The president's proclamation

On January 1, 1863, President Abraham Lincoln walked into his office in the White House in Washington, D.C. On his desk was a document called the **Emancipation** Proclamation, a declaration of freedom. The document said that slaves would be freed in the southern states that currently were **rebelling** against the **Union.** Lincoln had composed the document himself and written it out by hand.

Lincoln picked up a pen, dipped it in ink, and began to sign the document. As he did, his hand began to tremble. He did not have any doubts about signing the document, but he was aware of how important it would be. As he signed his full name at the bottom, he stated, "I never, in my life, felt more certain that I was doing right than I do in signing this paper."

## Rejoice!

In another part of Washington, D.C., Henry Turner, a church minister, waited with a crowd at the office of the *Evening Star* newspaper. As the copies of the Proclamation came off the press, everyone grabbed for one. Turner captured the third copy and ran through the streets to his church. He described what happened next:

This is the first of the four pages of the original Emancipation Proclamation. It was handwritten by President Lincoln.

4

"When the people saw me coming with the paper in my hand, they raised a shouting cheer. . . . I started to read the proclamation [but] I was out of breath and could not read. Mr. Hinton, to whom I handed the paper, read it with great force and clearness. . . . Men squealed, women fainted, dogs barked, white and colored people shook hands, songs were sung. . . . Great processions of colored and white men marched to and fro and congratulated President Lincoln on his proclamation. . . . It was indeed a time of times . . . nothing like it will ever be seen again in this life."

President Lincoln greets African Americans outside the White House on January 1, 1863. People all over the United States celebrated the announcement that slaves soon would be free.

## A first step toward freedom

The Emancipation Proclamation was written during the Civil War, a war between the northern and southern states. The document declared freedom only for the slaves in states that had rebelled against the Union, but it was the first step toward ending slavery.

# Slavery in the United States

## Before the Emancipation

Slavery was part of life in North America from almost the first days of the American **colonies.** In 1619, John Rolfe, a British settler in Jamestown, Virginia, bought twenty African slaves to work on his tobacco **plantation.** It was the first known sale of African slaves in what would become the United States of America. There were already thousands of African slaves in Central and South America, brought there by sailors from Portugal and Spain.

## Where did the slaves come from?

European sailors traded with the kingdoms along the west coast of Africa. They traded goods—such as cloth, guns, tools, and alcohol—for slaves. When trading goods did not buy enough slaves, they raided African villages. The African slaves came from many different groups, such as the Yoruba, the Konga, and the Fulani. They brought their various traditions and languages to this new land.

Slaves were brought mostly from the west coast of Africa. Ships from New England would carry rum and other goods to Africa to trade for slaves. The slaves would be taken to the West Indies and traded for molasses, which would be taken to New England and made into more rum. This system was called the Triangular Trade.

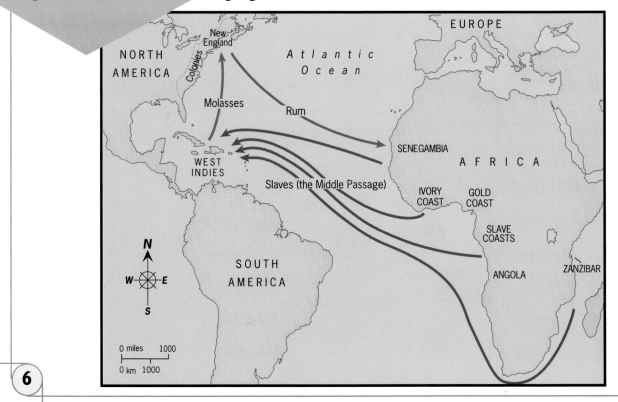

## No independence for slaves

When the U.S. won its freedom from the British by winning the Revolutionary War, many people thought the slaves would be freed, too. But southern states insisted that slavery remain legal. There were about 40,000 slaves in the North, or northern states, but there were more than 650,000 in the South, or southern states, where huge plantations kept large numbers of workers busy all year round. By the time of the **Emancipation** Proclamation, the number of slaves in the South had grown to more than 3.5 million.

A group of slaves sits on the dock at Jamestown, Virginia, having just arrived from Africa on a slave ship. They would soon be sold to a plantation owner.

### THE MIDDLE PASSAGE

As many Africans as possible were crammed into slave ships for the long weeks of the voyage across the Atlantic Ocean known as the Middle Passage. On most ships, Africans were nearly starved and kept in filthy conditions. Many were chained or branded with a hot iron. Between 10 and 40 percent of them might die during the voyage. A rare account of the Middle Passage is that of Olaudah Equiano, kidnapped from his village in Nigeria when he was a child. In 1789 Equiano wrote an autobiography that brought people's attention to the horrors of slavery. Describing the Middle Passage, he said, *"The shrieks of the women and the groans of the dying rendered the whole scene a horror almost inconceivable."*

# Division Between North and South

## Different ways of life

In the mid-1800s, most people in the United States still lived on farms, but in the North, many people were moving into cities. In cities, people produced goods in factories for their living. As the North became more and more **industrialized,** it became richer.

This painting shows slaves at work harvesting and processing cotton. Slaves worked in all kinds of jobs, but most were workers on the large cotton and tobacco **plantations** of the South.

Many northerners saw slavery as morally wrong. Some slaves in the North were freed, but in the South where the economy and lifestyle depended on slave labor, slave owners were not about to free their slaves. Wealthy southerners believed it was their right to own slaves. Even poor white southerners who did not own slaves supported slavery. As long as there were slaves, the poor whites were not at the bottom of the social order.

## A slave's life in the South

Being a slave meant being the property of another person, like a piece of furniture. Southern slaves usually lived in shacks with dirt floors. They were given little food and often grew their own. They got up at dawn, worked until sunset and sometimes they were whipped for disobedience. It was actually against the law to teach a slave to read or write. Even worse, their owners could sell them, breaking up families and taking children from their parents.

## Blacks in the North

Life was not easy for free blacks in the North either. Few white northerners thought that blacks should have equality with whites even if they disagreed with slavery. Some free blacks managed to prosper, but most were confined to low-ranking jobs and **segregated** from whites. If they were caught without the papers that said they were free, they could be sold back into slavery.

## Dreams of freedom

Before the **Emancipation** Proclamation, generations of slave families were kept in captivity, ignorance, and misery with no hope of change, but a longing for freedom grew in the hearts of some slaves. Some tried to escape to the North. Others rose in **rebellion.** White southerners were terrified of rebellion and reacted brutally. In 1831, when the slave Nat Turner organized a rebellion, at least 100 innocent slaves were killed by slave owners in response.

A great horror of slave life was the auction block. There, slaves such as this family in Charleston, South Carolina, were put on display to be sold to the highest bidder. Family members could be separated and sold to different owners.

# Toward Emancipation

### First moves to ban slavery

Most people did not think much about the rights and wrongs of slavery before the late eighteenth century. The debates that led to independence from the British, however, planted ideas about freedom that would not go away. By the early 1800s, most northern states had banned slavery. The international slave trade, which brought slaves from overseas, was banned in 1808, but slavery itself remained legal.

Adding to the debates about slavery was the fact that the U.S. was growing. The nation was purchasing and settling more **territories** across North America, and some of these territories were entering the **Union,** or joining the U.S., as states. **Congress** needed to make decisions about whether or not to allow slavery in the new states.

### The abolitionists

The early 1800s saw the start of an organized **abolitionist** movement. Abolitionists preached that slavery was a sin against God. In 1833, the influential American Anti-Slavery Society was formed. The society produced literature and sent speakers out to lecture about the cruelties inflicted on slaves. It pressured religious and political leaders to help them put an end to the practice of slavery.

In 1828, a young journalist named William Lloyd Garrison decided to devote his life to ending slavery. In 1831, he began publishing the *Liberator,* a weekly newspaper dedicated to the cause.

## Influential voices

One important abolitionist was Frederick Douglass, an escaped slave. His strong character and powerful arguments convinced many people that slavery was wrong. Another strong voice was that of Sojourner Truth. Despite never receiving a formal education, she inspired others with her dynamic personality and speeches against slavery.

Sojourner Truth was born a slave in New York but was freed when that state banned slavery in 1828. Like many abolitionists, she was deeply religious. Truth believed God had called her to fight for equality for slaves and women.

### *UNCLE TOM'S CABIN*

In 1852, Harriet Beecher Stowe published a book called *Uncle Tom's Cabin*. Although it was a work of fiction, it was so moving that many white people accepted the harsh reality of slavery for first time. The story of the brave, heroic slave Eliza and the gentle, loyal Uncle Tom who died at the hands of his owner brought support to the cause of abolition. It is said that when Harriet Beecher Stowe visited Abraham Lincoln in the White House during the Civil War, he greeted her by saying, "*So you're the little lady who started this great big war.*"

# The Division Grows

## The Missouri Compromise

In 1820, the **Union** was made up of eleven slave states in the South and eleven free states in the North.

Because the **territory** of Missouri wanted to join as a slave state, Congressman Henry Clay from Kentucky suggested a compromise. Missouri could be a slave state, but Maine would be a free state, keeping a balance between North and South. The Missouri Compromise also said that any new states south of the **latitude line** 36°30' would join the Union as slave states. In new states north of that line, slaves would not be allowed.

## Further efforts

The Missouri Compromise line did not apply to the territories in the west, however. In the following years, there would be many arguments between North and South about the spread of slavery into the west. In 1850, again with the help of Henry Clay, **Congress** worked out another compromise.

One of the most influential politicians in the history of the U.S. was Henry Clay. He was involved in most important decisions in the 1800s. He worked on both the Missouri Compromise and the Compromise of 1850.

The Compromise of 1850 included two new laws in addition to settling the dispute over the western territories. One, to please the North, made the buying and selling of slaves in Washington, D.C., illegal. The other, to please the South, was called the **Fugitive** Slave Law. This new law said that anyone who refused to help capture escaped slaves could be punished. Nobody was very pleased, however, and northerners and southerners continued their bitter disputes about slavery as more territories became states.

## The Dred Scott decision

Dred Scott was a slave from Virginia who had been taken by his owner to Illinois and Wisconsin Territory. After his master died, Scott claimed in the United States **Supreme Court** that he should be freed because he had lived for five years in those free areas, but the Supreme Court ruled that blacks had no rights at all because they were not citizens. It also ruled that it was **unconstitutional** for Congress to pass laws, such as the Missouri Compromise, prohibiting slavery anywhere. The Dred Scott decision divided the country even more.

One guide, or "conductor," on the Underground Railroad was former slave Harriet Tubman (left). She helped more than 300 slaves escape and stated proudly that she never lost a "passenger."

### THE UNDERGROUND RAILROAD

A number of **abolitionists** fought against the Fugitive Slave Law and risked punishment by helping slaves escape. The Underground Railroad was neither underground, nor a railroad. It was a secret organization of people who helped escaped slaves to get from the South to the North. They provided places to rest and help from one "station" to the next.

# Closer to Emancipation

## Desperate measures

After the Dred Scott decision, some **abolitionists** began taking the law into their own hands. In 1859, abolitionist John Brown raided an **arsenal** in Virginia, planning to get weapons to arm slaves. He and his followers were caught and executed, but the episode added to the fears of white southerners who were afraid that abolitionists were going to take away their slaves.

## A Republican president

As the election of 1860 approached, the two political parties competing to run the country had to choose their **candidates** for the presidency. Northerners and southerners in the Democratic party could not agree on their ideas about slavery. The party split into two, each with its own presidential candidate. The Republican party opposed the spread of slavery. It chose a lawyer named Abraham Lincoln as one of its party leaders.

After the outbreak of war, four more states seceded from the Union, bringing the total to eleven. Only four slave states, known as the border states, chose to stay loyal to the North. A large section of Virginia refused to secede, and it became the state of West Virginia in 1863.

CANADA

OREGON

WASHINGTON TERRITORY

DAKOTA TERRITORY

MINNESOTA

WISCONSIN

MICHIGAN

VERMONT

MAINE

NEW HAMPSHIRE

NEW YORK

MASSACHUSETTS

RHODE ISLAND

CONNECTICUT

NEBRASKA TERRITORY

IOWA

PENNSYLVANIA

NEW JERSEY

UTAH TERRITORY

COLORADO TERRITORY

KANSAS

ILLINOIS

INDIANA

OHIO

WEST VIRGINIA

DELAWARE

MARYLAND

Washington, D.C.

VIRGINIA

CALIFORNIA

MISSOURI

KENTUCKY

NORTH CAROLINA

Pacific Ocean

NEW MEXICO TERRITORY

PUBLIC LAND

INDIAN TERRITORY

ARKANSAS

TENNESSEE

SOUTH CAROLINA

Fort Sumter (Charleston)

Atlantic Ocean

MISSISSIPPI

ALABAMA

GEORGIA

TEXAS

LOUISIANA

FLORIDA

Gulf of Mexico

N
W E
S

Union states

Confederate states

State admitted to the Union, 1863

Border states

United States territories

MEXICO

0 miles 500
0 km 500

Confederates opened fire on Fort Sumter with cannons from the shore. You can see the cannonballs landing and exploding inside the fort in this picture. After almost two days of bombardment, the fort surrendered.

With the Democratic vote split between North and South, Abraham Lincoln was elected easily. He said that he would not interfere with slavery where it already existed, only to keep it from spreading, but the South did not believe him. In December 1860, before Lincoln was even sworn in as president, South Carolina **seceded** from the **Union.**

## The Confederacy

Six other states seceded shortly after South Carolina. They formed a group of states called the "Confederate States of America." Jefferson Davis was chosen as their first president. **Congress** declared that states could not secede from the Union and vowed not to tolerate any act of violence against the U.S. On April 12, 1861, however, Confederates, also called "**Rebels,**" bombarded Fort Sumter in South Carolina. Lincoln responded by gathering an army. The Civil War had begun.

### LINCOLN AND SLAVERY

President Lincoln made no secret of his personal view that slavery was wrong, but he said, "*My paramount [main] object in this struggle is to save the Union, and is not either to save or to destroy slavery.*" Lincoln said that if he could reunite the country by keeping slavery, he would. He also realized most northerners would not support the Civil War if it was being fought to free slaves. As the war progressed, though, Lincoln changed his mind. He became convinced that the war could not be won unless slavery was **abolished.**

# A Reason to Fight

## The Civil War begins

When the Civil War began, both the North and the South believed they would win easily. The first major battle, the First Battle of Bull Run in Virginia in July 1861, was a shock to both sides, but especially to the North, which lost the battle. Almost 900 men were killed in the fighting, and thousands more were injured. It was suddenly clear that the war would be long and bloody.

Lincoln (third from left) discussed the Emancipation Proclamation with his **cabinet** in July 1862. Most cabinet members agreed it was not yet time to make the announcement.

## A shift in attitude

The Confederates continued to win battles. At the same time, more Northerners were becoming convinced that slavery was wrong. Many, including President Lincoln, saw a practical as well as a moral advantage to freeing slaves in the South. The work of slaves helped support the Confederate Army. A proclamation freeing slaves could remove that support from the **Rebels** and give it to the **Union.** It would also win the support of the United Kingdom and France because both countries were firmly against slavery.

## Lincoln decides about emancipation

Lincoln was becoming convinced that this war was really about slavery, but he worried about what the border states would do if slaves were freed. If the border states went over to the Confederacy, the added strength might be enough to defeat the Union. Lincoln reached a decision. He would free only the slaves in areas controlled by the Rebels.

Lincoln waited for the right time. On September 22, 1862, he issued a Preliminary **Emancipation** Proclamation. It stated that, unless the Confederate states returned to the Union before January 1, 1863, all of their slaves would be "then, thenceforward, and forever free."

Union forces poured across Antietam Creek to attack the Confederates in the Battle of Antietam in 1862. When the Rebels withdrew, it was not a great victory for the Union. It was important, though, because until then the South had looked much stronger than the North. The Rebel retreat gave Lincoln the advantage he needed to make his Preliminary Emancipation Proclamation.

## FIRST STEPS TO EMANCIPATION

During the Civil War, **Congress** passed several laws that led up to the Emancipation Proclamation.

| | |
|---|---|
| July 1861 | The First **Confiscation** Act said that slaves engaged in work that helped the Rebels could be seized by the Union. |
| March 1862 | Military personnel were prohibited from returning **fugitive** slaves to their owners. |
| April 10, 1862 | Compensation was offered to owners who freed their slaves. |
| April 16, 1862 | Slavery was **abolished** in the District of Columbia. |
| June 1862 | Slavery was prohibited in all U.S. **territories.** |
| July 1862 | All slaves whose owners supported the Confederacy were declared free. |

# The Proclamation

### Lincoln frees the slaves

In the **Emancipation** Proclamation, Lincoln pronounced the slaves in the Confederate states to be free. He advised freed slaves to avoid violence unless in self-defense, and to "labor faithfully for reasonable wages." He also welcomed them into the **Union** armed forces.

### Reaction in the North

In the North, thousands of people poured into the streets to celebrate. They sang songs, held parades, and gave speeches. Not everyone was glad, however. **Prejudice** against blacks existed in the North. And some **abolitionists** wanted slavery **abolished** in the Union states, too.

### Reaction in the South

Although slave owners did not tell their slaves about the Proclamation, many learned of it anyway. Escapes increased and more slaves rose up in **rebellion.** Slaves were not immediately freed because of the Proclamation, but it paved the way for further measures. The document stated to the world that ending slavery was a major goal of the Civil War.

Although this painting does not show a real event, it celebrates the Emancipation Proclamation. The woman in the carriage is a symbol of freedom, and President Lincoln is on the right, holding the Proclamation. In the background is the Capitol building, seat of the U.S. government.

# THE EMANCIPATION PROCLAMATION

Whereas on the 22nd day of September, A.D. 1862, a proclamation was issued by the President of the United States, containing, among other things, the following, to wit:

"That on the first day of January, A.D. 1863, all persons held as slaves within any State or designated part of a State the people whereof shall then be in rebellion against the United States shall be then, thenceforward, and forever free; and the Executive Government of the United States, including the military and naval authority thereof, will recognize and maintain the freedom of such persons and will do no act or acts to repress such persons, or any of them, in any efforts they may make for their actual freedom.

"That the Executive will on the first day of January aforesaid, by proclamation, designate the States and parts of States, if any, in which the people thereof, respectively, shall then be in rebellion against the United States; and the fact that any State or the people thereof shall on that day be in good faith represented in the **Congress** of the United States by members chosen thereto at elections wherein a majority of the qualified voters of such States shall have participated shall, in the absence of strong countervailing testimony, be deemed conclusive evidence that such State and the people thereof are not then in rebellion against the United States.

"Now, therefore, I, Abraham Lincoln, President of the United States, by virtue of the power in me vested as Commander-in-Chief of the Army and Navy of the United States in time of actual armed rebellion against the authority and government of the United States, and as a fit and necessary war measure for suppressing said rebellion, do, on this first day of January, A.D. 1863, and in accordance with my purpose so to do, publicly proclaimed for the full period of one hundred days from the first day above mentioned, order and designate as the States and parts of States wherein the people thereof, respectively, are this day in rebellion against the United States the following, to wit: Arkansas, Texas, Louisiana (except the parishes of St. Bernard, Plaquemines, Jefferson, St. John, St. Charles, St. James, Ascension, Assumption, Terrebonne, Lafourche, St. Mary, St. Martin, and Orleans, including the city of New Orleans), Mississippi, Alabama, Florida, Georgia, South Carolina, North Carolina, and Virginia (except the forty-eight counties designated as West Virginia, and also the counties of Berkley, Accomac, Northampton, Elizabeth City, York, Princess Ann, and Norfolk, including the cities of Norfolk and Portsmouth), and which excepted parts are for the present left precisely as if this proclamation were not issued. And by virtue of the power and for the purpose aforesaid, I do order and declare that all persons held as slaves within said designated States and parts of States are, and henceforward shall be, free; and that the Executive Government of the United States, including the military and naval authorities thereof, will recognize and maintain the freedom of said persons. And I hereby enjoin upon the people so declared to be free to abstain from all violence, unless in necessary self-defense; and I recommend to them that, in all cases when allowed, they labor faithfully for reasonable wages. And I further declare and make known that such persons of suitable condition will be received into the armed service of the United States to garrison forts, positions, stations, and other places, and to man vessels of all sorts in said service. And upon this act, sincerely believed to be an act of justice, warranted by the **Constitution** upon military necessity, I invoke the considerate judgment of mankind and the gracious favor of Almighty God. [. . .]

# Emancipation Begins

## The end of the war

During 1863 and 1864, the tide of the Civil War turned. The **Union** forces of the North, under the leadership of General Ulysses S. Grant, were able to defeat the Confederate forces of the South. On April 9, 1865, Confederate General Robert E. Lee surrendered to Grant. The Civil War was over.

As a result of the Emancipation Proclamation, thousands of former slaves in the South headed north, to find freedom and to support the Union Army in the Civil War.

## Assassination

President Lincoln's plans for reuniting the nation included the abolition of slavery. Slaves were to receive full rights as citizens, including the rights to vote and to hold **public office.** How far these plans might have gone remains unknown. On April 15, 1865, six days after the end of the Civil War, Lincoln died after being shot by John Wilkes Booth. Vice President Andrew Johnson took over the presidency.

## New rights

The **Emancipation** Proclamation had been issued as a war measure to help defeat the South. Because of this, it could not become law in the rest of the nation without an **amendment** to the **Constitution.** Instead, **Congress** passed three amendments to ensure the rights of African Americans. The Thirteenth Amendment in 1865 banned slavery anywhere in the United States, whereas the Emancipation Proclamation had only freed slaves in the **Rebel** states. The Fourteenth Amendment in 1868 made it illegal to deprive any citizen of life, liberty, or property unless the law allowed it. It said that every citizen had equal protection under the law. The Fifteenth Amendment in 1870 said it was against the law to deny any man the right to vote on the basis of race, color, or previous enslavement.

A U.S. infantry unit stands at ease during the Civil War. More than 180,000 African Americans served as soldiers for the Union Army. About 38,000 were killed in the fighting.

### AFRICAN AMERICAN SOLDIERS

The wording of the Emancipation Proclamation was a clear invitation for blacks to join the Union Army. They did by the thousands, both escaped slaves and freed men from the North. At first, most were put to work doing hard labor, but others were trained as soldiers. One of the most famous black regiments was the 54th Massachusetts Infantry. Many white northern soldiers did not want to serve alongside black soldiers. They thought blacks would be cowardly and that they just were not clever enough to handle the job. The outstanding bravery and ability of the 54th Massachusetts proved them wrong and helped pave the way for equality for blacks.

# Reconstruction

## Rebuilding the nation

After the war, the United States entered a period known as Reconstruction, meaning "rebuilding." This term reflected a need not only to reunite the nation, but also to rebuild American society so that there was a place for millions of newly freed black people.

The government realized that former slaves would need help adjusting to their new way of life. So, in 1865, **Congress** established the Bureau of Refugees, Freedmen, and Abandoned Lands—also known as the Freedmen's Bureau—to help. The Freedmen's Bureau provided food, temporary shelter, clothing, and medical care.

## Political Reconstruction

During Reconstruction, there were many disagreements within the **federal** government. President Johnson was from the southern state of Tennessee and had more sympathy for white southerners than for former slaves.

The Freedmen's Bureau only existed between 1865 and 1872. It founded over 4,000 schools to help freed slaves—both adults and children—learn to read, write, and do arithmetic. This photograph from the 1860s shows one of the Freedmen schools in Beaufort, South Carolina.

He tried to prevent Congress from extending citizenship to blacks. His efforts were unsuccessful.

Starting in 1867, Congress passed other laws, called the Reconstruction Acts, that forced state governments in the South to recognize the rights of African Americans. For the first time, African Americans were allowed to vote and to take **public office.**

## The end of Reconstruction

Reconstruction governments in the South worked hard to rebuild the economy and improve life for their many new citizens. Within a few short years, however, Reconstruction was over.

The Republican Party, unified by the **Emancipation** Proclamation, held power in the national government until 1884. But by 1877, white Democrats had regained control of southern state governments. Much of the work toward equality was soon undone.

During Reconstruction, hundreds of African-American men became government officials. Eighteen became Congressmen. The first African-American members of Congress are shown here. The group includes Hiram Revels (far left), who became the first African-American senator in 1870.

## CARPETBAGGERS

Many northerners went south during Reconstruction. Some intended to help the newly freed slaves. Others hoped to take advantage of the South's problems. Southerners disliked all of them, and called them "carpetbaggers" because some northerners arrived with their belongings in suitcases made from carpet. A few carpetbaggers grabbed all the power and money they could get. Most, however, came to teach, advise, and help in the rebuilding of the South.

# A Segregated Society

## Jim Crow laws

The white southern Democrats who regained control at a local level after Reconstruction were as determined as ever to deny rights to African Americans. By the early 1900s, they had **segregated** society in the South. Many southern states passed laws known as Jim Crow laws. White and black people were required to use separate schools and hospitals. Churches, restaurants, and transportation systems were segregated, too, as were many stores and theaters. The **federal** government looked the other way in hopes of restoring the **Union.**

Here, a white man and a black man drink from opposite sides of a segregated water fountain. Even 100 years after slaves were freed, there were still signs all over the south reading "Colored Only" and "Whites Only."

## SHARECROPPERS

After the Emancipation Proclamation, some southern blacks were able to find work as sharecroppers. Sharecropping was a system in which white landowners provided living quarters and supplies to workers in exchange for a share of the crops raised. Often, landowners took so much that the sharecroppers were no better off than they had been as slaves.

## Voting rights denied

The **Emancipation** Proclamation may have ended slavery, but white people still held the power in southern society. They did everything they could to prevent African Americans from gaining an equal place in society. Despite the Fifteenth **Amendment,** they found several ways to keep African Americans from voting. For example, in some places, local laws stated that only people who could read and write could vote. Few former slaves could read or write, and so they were prevented from voting.

## Separate but equal

Even the courts upheld the Jim Crow laws. In 1892, Homer Plessy was arrested for sitting in a "whites only" railway carriage. He was found guilty of violating segregation laws. Plessy appealed to the U.S. **Supreme Court,** saying he was entitled to equal protection under the Fourteenth Amendment. In 1896, in a ruling known as *Plessy vs. Ferguson*, the Supreme Court declared that separate facilities were legal as long as they were equal. They rarely were equal, of course, but this was hard to prove in court.

A secret, terrorist organization called the Ku Klux Klan was formed in 1866 to keep black people from voting and thus keep the whites in power. They attacked and murdered African Americans and burned down homes, churches, and schools. The terrorist group is still around in smaller numbers today.

# The Fight for Equality

## The NAACP

In spite of the **Emancipation** Proclamation, black citizens were still denied equal opportunities in the United States. In 1909, a group formed the National Association for the Advancement of Colored People (NAACP) to challenge **segregation** laws in the courts. They won several victories and forced the public to acknowledge the lack of progress made since the Emancipation Proclamation.

## Falling barriers

World War II helped to lower some barriers as black soldiers once again proved their bravery and skill. After the war, in 1948, President Harry Truman ordered the armed forces to **desegregate.** Baseball player Jackie Robinson was signed up by the Brooklyn Dodgers, the first time an African American had entered major league baseball. Then, in 1954, the **Supreme Court** ruled that "separate but equal facilities are [by their nature] unequal."

One of the NAACP's biggest victories was in education. In 1954, the Supreme Court said that schools had to be desegregated. When a white community in Little Rock, Arkansas, refused to comply, President Eisenhower sent in soldiers so that black students could enter the school with protection.

## The civil rights movement

Many people date the beginning of the **civil rights** movement to December 1955, when Rosa Parks was arrested in Montgomery, Alabama, for refusing to give up her seat on the bus to a white person. Martin Luther King Jr., at the time a young church minister, organized a **boycott** of the city's buses. For more than a year African Americans refused to ride the buses. This nonviolent protest achieved victory when the Supreme Court declared that Montgomery's bus segregation laws were **unconstitutional.**

Spurred on by this success, Dr. King and other civil rights leaders took their crusade throughout the South. They succeeded in gaining job opportunities and fair treatment from many businesses. In the 1960s, public opinion shifted in favor of the movement, and President John F. Kennedy gave his support to equal rights. Later, **Congress** passed the Civil Rights Act of 1964, banning segregation in the U.S.

Martin Luther King Jr., (front row wearing hat) marches with his wife, Coretta, in 1965. Marches and other nonviolent demonstrations were the backbone of the 1960s civil rights movement.

## WE SHALL OVERCOME

The American folk song "We Shall Overcome" became the anthem of the civil rights movement. It took its words from a 1901 hymn:

"*We shall overcome, we shall overcome,*
*we shall overcome some day.*
*Oh, deep in my heart, I do believe*
*we shall overcome some day.*"

# Room for Change

### Equal opportunity?

In 1965, **Congress** passed the Voting Rights Act, which struck down the Jim Crow laws that had restricted blacks' right to vote. It had taken more than 100 years since the **Emancipation** Proclamation for blacks to achieve legal equality with whites, but it seems the Emancipation Proclamation did not really bring about social equality for the descendants of African slaves.

In the United States, poverty is still more widespread among blacks than among whites. In 1991, the overall family income for African Americans was only 57 percent of that of white families. Sadly, **prejudice** still affects the lives of many Americans.

Some people feel that select communities continue to keep African Americans out of their stores, their clubs, or their neighborhoods. In some areas, African Americans still are more likely to be arrested and convicted of crimes than whites, and their prison sentences are often more severe.

In poor, black, urban communities it can still seem as if there are differing opportunities depending on the color of one's skin. Frustration at racial inequality erupted into riots in Los Angeles, California, in 1992. These people are watching their neighborhood burn after attacks on buildings during the riots.

## An enriched culture

The United States has benefitted as African Americans rediscover their **heritage.** Slaves brought from Africa were forbidden to follow any of their home customs. Emancipation turned that around. African art, music, and dance have inspired African Americans and now play a part in American culture.

Secretary of State Colin Powell (left) takes his oath of office in January 2001 while his wife and President George W. Bush watch. Powell, a former general and war hero, is admired for his bravery and wisdom, and his efforts to improve social conditions for people, regardless of race.

American society as a whole is richer because of the fight by African Americans to achieve equality. All Americans can admire the accomplishments of prominent African-American political and religious leaders. Women, Native Americans, and other groups have been inspired to fight for their own rights because of what African Americans achieved. Gaining true equality has proven to be a long, difficult road. Each step brings the dream closer, and the Emancipation Proclamation was one important step in achieving this dream.

### KWANZAA

The holiday Kwanzaa was created in 1966 by Dr. Maulana Karenga, a college professor who wanted to help African Americans preserve their African heritage. Kwanzaa is a weeklong celebration based on traditional African harvest festivals. Each day the participants focus on one of seven principles. These principles are unity, **self-determination,** collective work and responsibility, cooperative economics, purpose, creativity, and faith.

# Timeline

| | |
|---|---|
| 1619 | First slaves sold in the North American **colonies** |
| 1787 | Northwest Ordinance prohibits slavery in the Northwest **Territory** |
| 1789 | **Constitution** makes slavery legal in United States |
| 1808 | January 1—U.S. prohibits importation of slaves |
| 1820–1821 | Missouri Compromise passed |
| 1831 | William Lloyd Garrison begins publishing the *Liberator* |
| 1833 | American Anti-Slavery Society formed |
| 1850 | Compromise of 1850 including **Fugitive** Slave Law passed |
| | Buying and selling of slaves banned in Washington, D.C. |
| 1852 | *Uncle Tom's Cabin* published |
| 1854 | Republican Party formed |
| 1857 | **Supreme Court** decides on case of Dred Scott |
| 1859 | October 16—John Brown leads raid on **federal arsenal** |
| 1860 | Abraham Lincoln elected president |
| | December 20—South Carolina **secedes** from **Union** |
| 1861 | February—**Rebel** states form Confederate States of America |
| | April 12—Confederates bombard Fort Sumter |
| | July 21—First Battle of Bull Run |
| | July—First **Confiscation** Act |
| 1862 | March—Military personnel prohibited from returning fugitive slaves to their owners |
| | April 10—Compensation offered to owners who free slaves |
| | April 16—Slavery **abolished** in District of Columbia |
| | June—Slavery prohibited in all U.S. territories |
| | September 17—Battle of Antietam |
| | September 22—Preliminary **Emancipation** Proclamation |
| 1863 | January 1—Emancipation Proclamation goes into effect |
| 1865 | April 9—Confederate surrender brings end to Civil War |
| | April 14—President Lincoln shot (died April 15) |
| | Reconstruction period begins |
| | December 18—Thirteenth **Amendment** approved, officially freeing all slaves |
| 1866 | **Civil Rights** Act passed |
| | Ku Klux Klan formed |
| 1867 | First Reconstruction Act passed |
| 1868 | Fourteenth Amendment approved |
| 1870 | Fifteenth Amendment approved |
| 1877 | Reconstruction period ends |
| 1896 | *Plessy vs. Ferguson* establishes principle of "separate but equal" |
| 1909 | NAACP formed |
| 1954 | Supreme Court rules against **segregation** |
| 1964 | Civil Rights Act of 1964 passed |
| 1965 | Voting Rights Act passed |

# Glossary

**abolish** to put an end to something

**abolitionist** person committed to ending slavery

**amendment** official change or added definition made to the Constitution of the United States of America

**arsenal** collection of weapons

**boycott** refusal to buy something or use something, as a protest

**cabinet** group of statesmen who serve as advisors to the president

**candidate** person seeking to be chosen for an official position or job

**civil right** basic right of every citizen, such as freedom

**colony** settlement, area, or country controlled or owned by another nation

**confiscation** taking of goods by an official

**Congress** government of the United States. A Congressman or woman is an elected member of Congress.

**Constitution** document that states the basic principles and laws of the United States

**desegregate** to get rid of segregation

**emancipation** setting free from slavery

**federal** concerning the whole nation as opposed to separate states

**fugitive** escaped person running away from authorities

**heritage** something inherited from earlier generations that forms part of a person's culture, such as traditions, beliefs, and language

**industrialize** to change from a society based mainly on farming and nonmechanical production to one based on use of machinery for mass production

**latitude line** imaginary line that goes horizontally around Earth

**plantation** large farm where crops such as tobacco or cotton are grown and large numbers of people are employed as workers

**prejudice** judgment about something based on previously held ideas rather than real reasons, for instance dislike of someone for their skin color rather than for their actual qualities as a person

**public office** position of authority in government or other public role

**rebel** to fight against authority, law, or control. People who do this are known as rebels and their actions are called rebellions. The Confederates were called "Rebels" during the Civil War.

**secede** to leave or withdraw from a group

**segregate** to keep groups of people separate from each other

**self-determination** having control of decisions and choices in one's own life

**Supreme Court** highest law court in the United States that has the power to make final decisions on legal matters

**territory** area of North America in the eighteenth century outside the actual states but owned and settled by the United States

**unconstitutional** going against the rules and principles of the Constitution

**Union** another name for the United States of America. When territories belonging to the U.S. became states, this was called "joining the Union."

# Further Reading

Carey, Charles W. *The Emancipation Proclamation.* Chanhassen, Minn.: Children's World, Inc., 1999.

January, Brendan. *The Emancipation Proclamation.* Danbury, Conn.: Children's Press, 1997.

Stein, R. Conrad. *Emancipation Proclamation.* Danbury, Conn.: Children's Press, 1998.

# Index